The Advent of Purple Madness

On a northwest wind,
a faint oaky perfume
of campfires and moldering leaves.
The woman senses my withdrawing,
nodding to the beckoning finger
of a temptress.
Tardily I obey regularities
of naggingly inadequate work,
struggle with hysteric dreams,
stare longingly, inexplicably
toward the distant wood,
attuned to seductive blue chords
from the lyre of the hunt goddess.
Unbidden I look up from my desk
when slanting rays give way to dusk
and big deer nose out from edges to feed.
My rifle has been rammed clean with powder solvent;
its banana fragrance pausing.
A full moon parts the fluff
of November nights,
dimpling forest floors with vanilla puddles
which melt beneath the wary hooves
of heavy-antlered bucks.
It is the advent
of purple madness,
of lilac isolation.

From Its Farthest Corners

For years I have ventured into gardens
of hemlock, birch, and aspen
beside rivers flowing so clear
that a man who looks hard enough
can see his soul
in their gray green depths.
I have tendered an arc of fly line,
mere half of perfection's circle,
and then laid it whispering flat onto moving streams,
hoping that a mighty trout will be fooled
just long enough to take the fly
and, in that second,
set before me deliverance.
I have tried to read the burble and ripple of brooks,
and their still places,
tried to mark the pages where speckled fish lie,
to underline the psalms they write
with rhythmically undulating tails
in lands where mountains frame far horizons
and skies are big enough for a man's rebirth.
A longing, incompletely understood,
draws me to distant waters.
On the back of a car,
a chrome symbol, shaped like a fish,
offers a clue.

Dawn on the Rimrocks

Oyster light
dilutes the stars
giving night time to escape
over the western range.
Sunfire soon will burnish
gray-white rimrocks.
A flitting chickadee
stares through
its burglar mask.
Far below, a truck growls
on the Collbran Road.
Down at Hittle's farm
a cow complains at the weight of a full bag.
A magpie chirs.
A raven croaks *arc arc* in the half light;
its wings *whit whiting.*
From an hidden draw, an elk's thrilling whistle.
Pinions emerge from amorphous darkness.
Mule deer tiptoe warily
into fields to browse.
There will be killing today,
but for now dawn
comes in peace
to the rimrocks.

Turning on High Final

After Bill died,
I went to the flying field
where we launched so many missions.
The wind was straight down the runway.
Just a touch of right rudder
would have held her true as an arrow.
The sky was as clear and blue
as an aviator's dream.
The rows of olive recon ships are gone.
Weeds have punched up
through age-dimpled taxiways.
I listened in vain for
a Lycoming engine coughing to life.
I closed my eyes and saw
Bill's white scarf trailing
in the slipstream.
He wore it saluting
World War I pilots who
rode the high hallways like knights.
There was a full choir
for Bill's funeral.
He'd have preferred
a Royal Street marching band
and spent the organist's fee
on a keg of beer
for his flying buddies.
We used to take bets on how high
our ships would climb
before gasping for breath in thin air.
Today, Bill, you collect the bets.

The Battle Afar Off

Her dancer's body
scalded my blood that September
we shot doves in Tamulipas.
Our eyes waltzed at arm's length.
We talked without touching.
Now it was ending.
The van sped through the night
toward a Texas border town.
She slept, head on her husband's shoulder.
Only the driver and I were awake, my hand
inches from the woman's bare neck,
my fingertips electric with longing,
I could have brushed her skin
without waking her.
Her perfume flared my nostrils.
I kept rehearsing how I would save her
if we wrecked or serve her
by some other gallantry.
Dawn grayed the eastern sky; a full moon
slid low: a fool's moon.
The sun fought to gain its throne
behind a towering thunderhead.
Egrets clustered like white suppositions
on the black loam of a sorghum field.
Startled, they struggled into the sky
and my dream came to pieces.

The Bowhunter

In this steamy September
archery season, a month before
rifle thunder flinderates the forest calm,
alerting watchful landowners,
he has slipped onto another man's farm
to poach deer, still in their summer tan,
grazing unafraid among the amplitude of sweetgum,
sassafras, and tulip poplar.
Now, he is in a booth at the 96 truck stop cafe
amidst the redolence of frying hash browns,
hamburgers grilled to greasy gray,
trucker-exhaled cigarette smoke,
the clamor of shouted orders and cookware,
and a pall of country western juke box blues.
His hair, long and yellow as Custer's,
cascades from a brimmed, camouflage hat.
He has worn his hunting garb
like a young private, fresh from basic training,
will come in full uniform
back to the high school dance.
The bowhunter's face cants toward the young girl
beside him, their food untouched.
I cannot hear what he whispers,
but, God, how I covet
the rapt attention in her eyes.

Midnight Smoke

The old man found the signs:
a sapling stripped of bark and bent
by slashing, velveted antlers,
black pellets glistening like oiled hematites,
earth scraped bare by cloven hooves.
The great animal which did these
would return.
The man climbed a tree to wait.
The slightest movement,
the merest clink of metal on button
or scratch of wool on pine bark
would send big deer bounding away.
An hour passed since dawn sifted grudgingly
through gray clouds,
then two.
He waited motionless while rain
soaked his shirt.
There: the faintest tick of hoof on leaf.
The old man turned,
heart thundering in his chest.
Through dense sweetgums, a hint
of gray brown hide, moist black nostrils,
thick, buff colored antlers.
The man raised his rifle.
With instincts from before recorded time
the deer sensed the man
and vanished like midnight smoke.
The old man nodded,
acknowledging a superior being.

Bowls of Mixed Wine

A cock urges the world awake
at the impossible hour of 4 a.m.
A great horned owl booms
its incessant question
through the woods:
Who cooks for you?
Like a jewelry heist gone awry
loose diamonds have spilled
across the sky.
It is time to rouse the other men
before turkeys leave their roosts
in pearl dawn,
but first, my daily reverie
of you.

Enough of Alien Gods

There is a longing for the hills.
I look about my treasures,
recounting all my pleasures, yet still
there is a longing for the hills.
I have bayed at the spoor of fame,
but lost it; thirsted for power,
but never sipped its secret spring.
Love I found pretty
as a thistle and just as hard to grasp.
There is a longing for the hills.
My feet want to know the contour lines
of ridges, the grassy slant of fields.
I yearn to live beyond the memory
of clocks, to march in step
with days and seasons.
I want to watch fall torch the woods,
winter hide their shame,
and spring bring them fresh linen.
I want away from computers, phones, and FAXs
because I have this longing for the hills.
I want to smell camp smoke tendrils
on cool mornings, passing skunks,
and the musk of foxes.
I want to hear raindrops tapping on my tent, the snap
of branches under hoof, the *cawr* of crows, and
the tremolo questions asked by owls.
I want to touch a trout's sleek, dappled skin and feel
the wet bark of oaks and sweetgums
where they grow in such abundance
in the hills.
In the midst of daily working
which I've learned to do so well
I find myself daydreaming, ever
longing for the far enchanting hills.

Wapiti

Hooves resonating thunder.
Then gasping breaths
like winded cavalry mounts
charging through junipers in pearl dawn.
They jump, twanging
barbed wire like cheap bedsprings.
Two cows; a majestic bull, dominating
despite his hard run,
a titan filling the horizon.
Brown heaving hide fills my gunsight.
Time stops; elk and man fuse
in red flame.
He runs, weaves, thumps hard in the meadow,
ebbing crimson.
His eyes die last
neither angry
nor afraid.

As Stubble before the Wind

The day began on salamander legs
the minutes taking little splay-footed steps
while the baying of hounds wafted like smoke
uphill to our cabin.
There was time to visit sections of red oak,
my mall *ponking* futilely until it sensed
a parting of atoms where a seam waited to form
then struck deep with a *thwack*
like bone giving way to fist.
There was time to arc an earthworm
over the breeze-rumpled lake;
the filament glinting in the sun;
like a silver tracer round falling short,
plooping harmlessly into the water.
We needed two trout for dinner
and conquered our greed to take more.
There was time for hungry pruning saw teeth
to feed on rhododendron, laurel, and hemlock stems
which had advanced their civilizations across the path
we once walked at twilight
and will again when I can drive
their phalanxes back to pre-war boundaries.
It was a day everything had meaning
and understandable endings.
It was a day when I questioned
returning to the city
wedging my feet into tight shoes,
choking my neck with a tie,
and living days seldom
like this one.

The Work of Our Hands

We found the tornado-blasted red oak in deer season.
My brother and I returned in January
to claim it for our hearths.
We shifted into four-wheel drive;
howling engines elbowed past saplings
and soldier briars whipping, snagging,
and screeching on fenders.
The chain saw snorted to life, coughing smoke,
growling in a blizzard of sawdust,
amputating precise sections of trunk.

He taught me to raise the splitting mall
with back muscles, conserving the power
of my forearms; let the solid steel head
work in the downstroke; don't flail
with wild, roundhouse swings like a boy
showing off for his sweetheart at the fair.
Look right at the spot you want to hit.
The wood rent asunder at a single stroke
as if lightning lived in our arms.
We fell into a gandy dancer's rhythm:
one brother holding the wood for the other;
taking turns with the mall.

On this snow-crusted day,
brothers joined as primal gatherers,
coming as close to speaking love
for each other as we could.
Passing new logs like artillery shells
for stacking; then breathing deeply
the rich, wine-cask smell
of fresh wood in the garage.

An Arm Too Short to Save

My work gloves scratch down into moldy straw
exposing earth-stained creeper networks.
Chrome bladed clippers snick and snip twice
so severed ends
won't reunite when I turn my back.
Prying tri-pointed green leaves
away gently to loosen their grip,
then putting my back into it:
ripping vines until they peel like zip open feed bags,
break above my head,
hang waving like stumps of a child's dreams
cut off by finger-wagging parental insistence
on realism and responsibility.
Even greater my terrible satisfaction
if hairy shoots have bitten
into bark and chunks of pine come away
like brown scabs.
Saw through pulpy hangers. Hear them snap
like a twined, sweat-glistening sumo wrestler
losing his hold.
Look down for broken stalks, sprung up,
hoping to reattach
like teen lovers surprised in the backseat
by the yellow sword blade of a cop's flashlight.
Look up to see the trunk outreaching
ivy and wisteria, soon to wither and brown,
in its climb for blue sky,
growing straight and tall as might a first-born son
free of reflexive, choking censure.

Let the Fields Be Jubilant

We went into the field, hoping
for doves. A lemon sliver sun
fought for birth among rain clouds.
Fog moved among us
like pale drapes of remembrance.
Jim and Bonnie wore camouflage,
sat half-concealed in the johnson grass.
Secluded, separated, hoarding our thoughts,
we waited for fast wings to appear
in the sky.
I might have shouted to them or
run to their hiding places,
but the rules demand isolation,
rooting my feet to the plowed soil.

More Profitable than Silver

The rod trembled in my vertical hand
like a two-year old mare at the Derby starting gate.
My forearm flashed down; the green floating line
whisked toward the lake's far bank
invisible in fog.
I drew in curls of line giving a darting motion
to the silver fly with orange and red hairs.
The trout took it as if a SCUBA diver, hovering
just below the fish-burbled surface,
had yanked the tiny lure with black-gloved hand.
Time after time my reel shrieked in protest
as the big rainbow swam powerfully
for the safety of deep water.
I fought him as one would an arm wrestler
over a barroom wager except here,
there was no cheering, odds-making, or pungent smell
of expensive cigars:
just two willful males locked in surreal, silent combat
in the cool, enshrouding mist.
The fish showed his pink, midline stripe,
his white underside.
He turned tail down, gathering
for a leap he was too tired to make, but
still humbling me with his body's daunting authority.
Finally he yielded to the net, filling it
with potency and might.

Like a Pent-Up Flood

If you happened upon it
walking through the forest, slapping
at mosquitoes and gnats from the Gum Swamp,
you might judge from the cheap blue tarpaulins,
cast off, sagging chairs, rope-and-sapling table,
and the acrid breath of still-warm ashes
that you had found an hobo village.
It is a place of release
where men yearning for control
yet falling short so often
at making what they do come out right
can bond in their common failure
to predict the secret habits and pathways
of thick-antlered whitetail deer.
In hunting camp all men are humbled
by their prey's caprice and eccentricity. Some say orneriness
as if the animals have a personal grudge,
a wish to torment
outside of staying alive.
Theories abound on the pull of the moon,
the coming and going of weather fronts,
whether to smoke in the woods,
the best rifle, the most powerful bullet,
what scents work best, what camouflage pattern
and what calls to blow.
Anecdotes fly back and forth, but
lasting truth is as evasive as finding a seat
where campfire smoke doesn't drift.
Hunters who cannot speak of a child gone bad,
eroded fortunes, or love unuttered and lost
willingly tell of the missed shot, the wounded quarry,
days of seeing only birds,
or neck hairs prickling when squirrels
prance on leaves like the nearing hooves
of ten-point bucks, of endless waiting,
lost equipment, and misery in drenching rain.
Perhaps it is an hobo camp after all
where men riding separate tracks pause,
give of what they can for an evening or two
before swinging aboard outbound boxcars,
the memories fading like lonely train whistles
into indifferent winter nights.

16

The Path of the Righteous

Snow fell hard at dusk,
flakes floating into the stream
like mayflies risen, mated, and died.
I almost didn't see the man,
camouflage jacket blending
with dark rhododendron and laurel.
His orange line curled back
in the classic arc, tensed, straightened,
whispered onto the surface
offering black strands woven like a cricket
to unseen trout.
He stood still as a stone but
for the rhythmic casting arm, sending
the line out again and again
visiting different lies in the creek
where salmonoid might wait, see, strike.
At last he yielded, reeled in,
went away into the gathering twilight,
his steps unhurried.
I yearned to be like him.

The Lion's Tale

Cancer like a lion
belly to the ground in flaxen grass,
padding on silent feet,
stalks us, the unwary herd.
Nervous, we stir, sensing unseen danger,
but the wind is with the lion.
We continue grazing.
Her yellow eyes know
which one she wants.
Like tawny fluid her charge.
Her victim, white eyes bulging, lunges, falls.
Drawn by the scent,
surgeons, like hyenas, rush in,
scatter stoop-shouldered vultures,
snip flesh, scrape bone,
slink off
with blood-smeared maws.
Atop the acacia, the vultures: leering, patient;
certain their turn
will be
next.

Dark Squadron

of black birds
diving, corkscrewing, zooming, wheeling,
ebon against a pink dawn.
Their cries like rustling
leaves plucked from the forest floor
and borne aloft
by a wind determined to blow them
far away.
Later, crows
paddle silently upwind
like gloomy little thoughts
transiting an optimist's day.
This cold morning, the sun
would rather nest in the pines, showing
only its rim
far too long.

To All Perfection a Limit

It is almost too much for three boys
holding down city jobs,
trying to make a trout refuge
on sweat-soaked weekends
in a Carolina forest.
Knee deep in creeks,
slapping at black flies
that leave welts
like rattler bites.
Mosquitos whining in for what skin
the flies don't claim.
Gnats whirling in our faces like retinal disease
and fire injecting hornets,
hovering in nests hidden in twisted laurel.
We hack at rhododendron tentacles, letting
sunlight onto the water so mayfly
and caddis larva will rise from rounded gravel
seeking brief lives out of water
and hungry fish will strike.
Unlike Jason, we cannot find Medusa's head.
We chop at her rhododendron hair,
hearing planty laughter when we have to leave.
Much will grow back
before we return.
This is work for hired men, but hired men
come back to poach in the way of hill folk.
By Sunday we can see what we have done, more
than we can say most days
on our town jobs.
There's no quarterly evaluation,
no sucking up to presidents here.
Amidst men who make a living taking
there is something here of putting back,
of planting without harvesting,
as if in this one remote place
something lost can be regained.
A dream, perchance a fantasy,
but dreams ennoble men who,
in deep woods, touch
the fingertips of God.

More Than Watchmen Wait

Through Sunday morning fog
my truck cab an isolated cocoon
in light traffic.
Motion, space, time.
Life within living.
A trip inside the trip.
Crows rise from roadkills,
cruise briefly above the windshield
like dolphins on a bow wave.
A shrouded sun shows
half a yellow tongue as if God
tasted a green persimmon.
The truck runs north, steady
as a horse knowing the way home.
My mind turns off at side roads, wanders
into small towns with ridiculous names.
I have not learned what I wanted to know, only
a few things I didn't, but there are miles
yet to go.

Finding Mr. Right

His guns will be immaculate.
Peering down the barrels
pointed toward a bright light
almost will blind you.
His kitchen will look like the Waffle House grill
just before shift change
on Christmas Day.
When you mention dust as a verb
he will stare at you
without comprehension.
His ties aren't likely to match his suits
but his camping stuff will be arranged
like a sporting goods store.
Your dog will come wagging to him unbidden
as will your children
and probably your cat.
He will beg off taking you dancing,
yet if you have a secret mountain to climb
pack your gear.
Despite the impudent bumper sticker
on his pickup,
you will sense his reverence
when he enters the forest.
He may not know your current movie swoon.
Ask him to name the stars in heaven
on a cloudless winter night.
He will shoot dove and quail
without a qualm,
but plunge over his waist into an icy stream
to save a sluggish trout worn down
by the fight.
You probably won't get flowers from him.
He'll bring firewood, venison, and pheasant.
When you finally decide to let him kiss you,
it will feel as if he means it.
He will be hard to rope and tie.
Like a wild thing, you will feel freedom
shiver beneath his back
when your hand
touches his bare flesh.

Waking in Colorado

Horses whipped into foamy lather,
the sun chariot comes early to this Colorado valley,
this last dip in the road
before the jagged peaks west of Vail and Kremmling.
On sloughs left by spring floods
gold shimmers like cream suspended
above dark liqueur.
A jet draws pink pencil lines
in pearl sky.
Canada geese call the morning roll
braying their two-note complaint
like a rusted barn door hinge,
a beginners' violin class.
Here the river from which the West drinks
slides placidly like a sinuous, well-fed serpent,
past green willows and fat cattle,
hinting not of future savagery
in the Grand Canyon.
I have come to tempt heavy trout
from its gray waters,
to find peace in the tug of current
against my waders.
Now, waking in Colorado, I stand long
at the window,
baptized in waves of awareness,
wondering yet again
why I have lived so much of life
beyond the reach of rivers.

Generation of the Upright

Sneaking away from tennis chatter,
the hostess showed me the lake path
among ripening rhododendrons
to a weathered boathouse where her timber baron father,
had fished at evening,
teaching a carefree girl the channels
where the big ones loiter.
Now she goes to the lake
when life stops making sense
as it too often does.
I slid the old canoe onto burnished water,
gliding in the windless dusk like a dream.
The mirror surface erupted:
tiny missiles breaking water, showing white underbellies,
speckled sides, flopping back into the deep, unable,
for all their trying, to change places
with the dipping bullbats, to swim in air.
I caught and released fingerlings
before a savage strike ripped
my floating white and brown fly.
The fish fought with authority, showing
amber and red whorls in the net
and scarlet centered fins, a native brook trout,
lineage predating the red men
who gathered in these foreboding woods.
Freed, he looked once at me without gratitude,
rolled, departed.
Back at the house, dinner well in progress,
guests stare at a man
who would pass up the cocktail hour,
to go alone onto the lake in the night.
On the wall, the baron had mounted
a brookie about the size of mine,
legacy of the sporting way.
I felt his touch,
saw his nod approving.
His daughter was the only one
who caught it,
understood
with misty eyes.

In Zeal as in a Cloak

Bushily bearded hunters
have memorized that October Saturday
prophesied months ago
as opening day of deer season.
They have eased into hardware stores,
tried the patience of dutiful clerks
with last year's best hunting yarns,
bought big game licenses
and toyed with the clink
of shiny, brass-jacketed ammunition.
Skinning knives are honed like razors
on stones dampened with butternut-scented oil.
Ramrods slide through long-barreled rifles
and anxious fingers test the metallic snap of triggers.
They have rubbed mildew off boots
left sleeping through the summer in closets,
made excuses to their wives,
begged off grandchildren's soccer games,
plunked down cash like the desperately ill
for musk and lures "guaranteed" by cunning vendors
to bring trophy bucks within spitting distance.
They've heaved bulky tree stands into eager pickup trucks,
stocked up on fat sausages and other diet taboos,
stashed a casual six pack or two,
and are trying for a night's sleep
free of hunting nightmares.

Before the appointed day, the woods
are quiet, inauspicious, uneventful:
like being in Bethlehem one night early,
bearing no gifts,
encountering no angels,
seeing no star in the east.

My sleep, too, is troubled
as dream deer flash like gray blankets
waved amidst towering hardwoods
offering no clear shot.
Like the others, I wait with knotted stomach
and shallow breath
for the annual miracle,
the visceral, atavistic portent,
of opening day.

Looking upon Their Nakedness

Paddling upwind on dawn's apricot daiquiri edge
like ebony sidewheelers
settling raucously into the tops
of lordly pines: crows.
They enter the forest as boisterously
as a truck full of stubble-chinned deer stalkers,
tanked up on the liquid cardboard of truck stop coffee,
black as the heart of a faithless wife.
Two of the men perfume the cab
with the fruity musk of last night's
Jack Daniels and Coke.
Theirs the happiness born of hope
and common enterprise: the crows seeking grain;
the men
identity.

Instead of Briers the Myrtle

The developer says a dirt road
hurts property values,
stifles new subdivisions,
but you can't see where deer
have crossed an asphalt highway.
Red clay trails that ramble into the country
want to be named when men lay down macadam.
Next will come house numbers.
When the pavers have finished, no more fishtailing,
wheels spinning,
tossing up rooster tails of gummy mud.
A blacktop road doesn't shine under a full moon
or change from dusty rose to crimson at dawn.
Tires will run smoothly on a proud highroad,
but I will miss
the music of gravel, the chalky smell of dust
coming in through the vents.
It won't feel right stopping in the middle of a hardtop pike
to talk to my neighbor coming the other way.
We'll be in too much of a hurry to wave.
Too much that is right
will find an indecent grave
under the pavement.

A Mountain Unscaled

On a cloudless night
I want to linger by the roadside,
come to terms with terror lingering
just inside the treeline,
held at bay by the half moon.
I need to open my palm to candent light,
loosen my grip on future fears,
watch them melt like blackberry sherbet.
The road turns, my shade walks beside me,
the furniture of memories
too long sat in.
Something hurries me along.
Another night perhaps.
The mountain unscaled
is patient.

The Poaching Hour

The news travels faster than rumors of war
or thunder along the backs of southern mountains
when the trout stocking truck trundles
to private ponds in Jackson County.
Old man Henry's bought fish; word crackles
at jet speed over rural phone lines,
reaching the farthest community beyond Sylva
before the last hatchery rainbow wriggles down the chute.

It is a call to the time-honored poaching rite,
clear and galvanizing
as a hunter's horn summoning hounds
to a fox's pungent trail.

Night-creeping bearded men with bad teeth
slither among laurel and rhododendron
in the dark of the moon
whisking earthworms over the mirror surface
of Henry's lake, waiting like spiders
for tug on filament line, listening
with cat ears for crunch of warden's boot.

Cuckolding the land owner means as much
as sneaking his fish.
There's extra delicacy to a filched trout,
a piquancy conveyed
by the post-midnight adventure.

Men and boys who wouldn't lift a dime
from a cash drawer
or cross a property line in broad daylight
break into sweat waiting among the trees
for the poaching hour.

The Wicked Not Forsaken

Summer licks the bitter milk
of fall,
recalls the delicate, misty hair of forest,
the white fluff of moon
above languid black water.

Winter smells fat sausage chains cooking,
lusts for the lucent silk of snow,
wind's shadow language,
the weak egg boil of sun,
raw iron stare of rain,
swift knives of sleet.

Only death thinks of music.

My Pickup

Just a mid-life crisis
she sniffed at bridge club
amid condescending nods.

Sooner or later a man needs to answer
the cries of untamed places
wailing from his deepest heart.
A truck can take him there correctly.
He's getting close when the song
of off-road tires on blacktop gives way to crunching gravel
and scents of pine and new grass come in
the lowered window.
You don't see air fresheners or lacy curtains
with bobbing tassels
in a pickup.
It won't be citified.

Like an unbroken mustang,
it wants to gallop for the hills the moment you forget
to close the fence gate.

Watch men passing in trucks
lift one or two fingers from the steering wheel:
a fraternity sign
among the properly initiated.

No, my dear, the crisis
is that I waited until mid-life
to buy one.

The Rabbit's Fear

I measure the seasons by my neighbor.
In fall, his olive green tree climber comes off
an orange wall bracket.
The whitetail buck best be wary.
In January, his mud-spattered truck
mutters out, the black rubber hand grip
of his battered splitting maul leaning
against his chainsaw.
Time to gather and cleave pungent red oak
for fires.
In February, I find brown-barred and gray feathers
from bobwhite quail on his asphalt drive.
In March, a rasping screech, like fingernails
raking a blackboard, slithers through the firewall.
He's practicing his turkey call.
In May, the whistling line of his fly rod
loops in a graceful U before him,
behind him, straightens, lands on the grass
light as a mayfly. I know that rainbow trout
have begun to rise.
Sometimes women ease pricey sedans
into his garage, seldom the same one
twice or thrice, often leaving
before dawn.
I wondered aloud why he had not
taken a wife, settled down like his neighbors.
He glanced at me before shrugging, saying
it never seemed to be
the right season,
but the brief look in his eyes
made me know the rabbit's terror
in a wolf's amber glare.

Flying School

You would have loved that little yellow plane, too.
It strapped on like
a menopausal bachelor's roadster.
Starting the riding mower engine
shook the fabric and metal frame,
blew oil and rubber fumes back into
the two-seat cockpit.
Jouncing over hazy Texas fields and villages
in washboard summer skies,
pulling the stubby nose up, up
until it blocked the sun,
kicking over into a spin,
recovering,
gliding in to bouncy fledgling landings.
We marveled at being paid
to play among birds,
believed all women worshipped us
and that we lived
beyond the reach of gods.

The Cup of Wrath Drained

Tan and white it sprawls
on the black road, the too sweet whiff
of fresh blood pooling carmine
on yellow centerline.
A deer down on the highway,
legs askew never again to bound,
to float in air above fields.
This death so unwilling, so unwitting.

An elderly Ohio couple, car
catercornered in the lane,
emergency blinkers synchronized
with their bewildered eyes
flickering behind thick lenses.
This death of grace so public:
recorded by deputies and warden
in flashing blue light,
an item of official paperwork,
of insurance claims.

A passing hunter wonders whether
the doe came from the wood,
crossed the road,
to offer absolution.

When Jackals Grow Not Afraid

An old man lines his den
with mounted antlers, chapters
of his life afield.
Finally his grandchildren tire
of his hunting stories.
Just as well: the tales have begun
to run together.
When he forgets the details,
he stares numbly
at the blurred trophies, filmy eyes watering,
shaking his head.
The end of the hunt
is near
and circling jackals
grow not afraid.

By Ways They Have Not Known

December dusk catches a yardman
tardily at his chores.
Clipping privet, he
bends the willing gray stalks over his knee,
coils the pliant ends into tiny maces,
stuffs them into flapping brown paper bags.
A suspicious dog barks lustily
at the stranger making
curious night moves and sounds.
A woman looks out,
kitchen light flaring behind her.
Seeing it is only a workman, she shushes the dog,
turns back to the snapping grease
under frying chicken.
She looks nervous
as though men of good purpose
should not be about after dark.
The wifeless yardman smiles,
licks his lips at the chicken smell,
contemplates a cold supper,
an even colder bed.

Looking into Cars

It's 30 much of the way;
sometimes 25.
These snaking mountain blacktops,
bright with morning sheen,
give you time to see the faces
in oncoming cars.

Big sedans and off-road wannabe sport trucks
lean on their front shocks,
tires chirping on the yellow line,
yachting flags or country club logos
on the front plates,
drivers pushing it for early golf:
grim faced with pursed lips
so busy and scheduled even in retirement.

Working men come at me in pickups,
often with an injured fender or two,
sometimes a troubled grille,
back springs sagging under heavy equipment.
At the wheel, men in billed caps
show white teeth under black beards
when they smile
and wave back.

One Right Thing

The river's skin is gray with fatigue:
too many blue and red rafts
sagging with scantily clad, nubile sirens
and their beer-breathed, sunburned knights
have coasted down its back today, the last
arriving as deep shadows reach like phantom curtains
for the far bank.
I wade in, casting vainly for trout
scattered by rock-throwing, shrieking children
and barking dogs lustily chasing frisbees
tossed out from shore like shotgunned mallards.
A great blue heron glides toward a stump
like an injured heavy bomber desperately trying to land
on a tiny runway. With backpedaling wings
he somehow makes a full stop
without flopping off into the stream,
tucking beak in against breast
like an embarrassed pilot.
The last rays of steeply angled August light
forgivingly color him gold.
Strands of seaweed sweep down current
like green snake skeletons, some of them
catching my flies, bending my rod tip mockingly
as if a fish had struck.
Finally, it is over in that hour after the sun has set
but before there is enough of night
for the half moon to reflect on sliding water.
A hatch of midges boils up like dandruff flakes.
A swimming muskrat's head pops up
sampling the sudden quiet.
In these fecund moments of regained peace
I step back to shore with an empty creel
but the fullness of having done one right thing.

The Sound of Ancient Ruins

Far away in the night
a train rumbles
like the passage
of unfulfilled expectations:
loves found and lost,
guilt destructively cherished,
things dreamed but undone.

The diesel horn is as doleful
as my regrets.

I lie awake in my sleeping bag
under the mathematically perfect
pirouette of stars,
wondering whether worthy deeds,
strewn hither and yon like landmines,
can impede Gabriel's path.

Wealth from the River

Two of us study the flow charts
and call for the time when men at Buford Dam
will open penstocks to Lake Lanier
letting great ropes of water
roar over voltage-making turbine blades
bigger than houses.
We put our canvas-covered inner tubes
into the cold, green Chattahoochee River at Medlock Bridge
well ahead of water churning downstream from the dam
like a wild-eyed cavalry horse in a saber charge.
We calculate the time to the next boat ramp
and push out into the current, fly rods at the ready,
under a cool, cloudless sky.

The susurrus of cars overhead
on the concrete span of Route 141 subsides.
An astonishing quiet settles over us.
Suddenly, city-dulled ears
hear cawing crows, cackling mallards, braying Canada geese,
and the curiously irritable rasp of great blue herons.
A breeze dimples the surface bringing
the smell of new mown grass and the tang
of outboard motor exhaust.

There is an eerie sense of vulnerability
in easing beyond the reach of help,
of knowing no one on the bank could hear my shout
if the tube leaks air or I flip upside down
trying to stand at a shoal.
I try to keep Marvin's blue floater within sight
and hailing distance,
but the current pushes him ahead of me.

Our flylines search for trout near fallen logs and shady spots.
Other anglers who have dropped anchor
are like oases on trade routes
along the river's moving desert.
We ask about their luck and what the fish are taking
then slide on like two nomads in a caravan.
Serenity seeps like a cool breeze
into the innermost closets of my mind.

Finally, I stop looking at my watch.
When the rusted skeleton of the old Jones Bridge
comes into view around a bend, we will be there
and there is no need to contemplate it until then.
There will be no navigation error,
no requirement to keep revising our arrival estimate.

In the end, the river has its way with those who drift.
For an hurried man who wants to control life
and fortune and love,
that is something wanted.

And Kings to the Brightness

Young saplings stand in dense formation
ramrod straight in winter gray garb:
like military cadets
held too long at attention.
A westering sun, slipping fast
from its throne,
grants a parting favor.
Slanting rays touch them briefly with the gold
of lieutenant's bars
as you have gilded
the gray side of my heart.

Images of the Wind

My flourescent green fly
floated like a raisin
in a patch of amaretto and cream
left on the fast-darkening lake
in sunset's afterglow.
A striking fish broke the sheen of water,
but did not hold.

Later, I cast into the secret pool
of a woman's mind.
Her eyes considered my offering,
turned away,
but did not flee
into the shadowy hiding places
of panicked trout.

Who Takes Hold of Your Right Hand

Judging from the time he spent there fishing,
sometimes just staring out at the lake for hours,
I think my father found his soul on Royal Island.
As a child I loved playing in the sand in his shadow
while summer hours wore on.
As a teen I stopped going out there with him
because it was too quiet and so long
before he was ready to come home.
I was too juiced up to just sit out there and wait
when I could be driving around town, bobbing
to rock 'n' roll on the car radio,
and trying to peek down the girls' dresses.
As a man, driven by the job's merciless tempo,
I finally grasped his need for solitude
 among the windswept pines,
the agonizingly lonesome call of loons,
and the quiet passings of bull moose
wading above their knees, succulent weeds dangling
from their mouths like green handlebar mustaches.

My father wanted his ashes scattered
on the narrow island which pointed like a sandy finger
vaguely in the direction of Detroit
although there was no significance in its doing that.

When the day came, I had been gone so long
I had to get my brother to help me find
that isolated cove dad loved.
It seemed right to put part
of his ashes on shore and sift the rest like gray talc
onto the sparkling emerald water.

Mother wanted the same. She told us she regretted the time
dad needed to be off by himself on the island,
felt inadequate about it, hoped being with him there
at the end would cure that, would make them
inseparable like in love poems and her favorite movies.

Once again, brother and I picked our way to the cove
through thickets whose thorns snatched blood from our arms
when we tried to fend them off,
vines that made us duck and turn this way and that. To lighten
the sadness, we joked about how, as children, we had glided
through the brush like fawns wondering why it was so hard
for the old man to keep up with us.

I brought along my rod and, after we had offered mom's ashes
to the lake wind, a northern pike, bigger even
  than my memory of dad,
wrenched my lure. Fought like a whale.
It was the biggest fish I'd ever landed.

My brother said I'd have to release it
because pike season did not begin until tomorrow.
Release the trophy of a lifetime without even a photo?
But, like a dutiful son, I did.

Back at the dock, they said
that, actually, pike went into season
today.

To the Place of Its Setting

There are roads leading out of Cashiers.
Women speak of the blacktops
to antique shops in Highlands,
to flea markets in Pickens,
to the county seat in Sylva
where promises are notarized;
to Sapphire for society golf
and swishy tennis.
There are gravel tracks leading down
from high in the rounded Appalachians
bringing mountain men with brown teeth
to mow lawns and plow garden plots,
coveting stocked trout ponds,
as they work,
dreaming through cigarette-squinted eyes
of midnight poaching.
There are roads leading out of Cashiers,
this place content with the labor of a man's hands
and the curling cast of his flyline.
Dawn, not the coffee timer,
starts my day.
I don't wait up for the news; the news
is the goldfinch pair and the bluejays
which arrived from the north today,
the turkey that yelped
in the wood by the pond and the boy
who wrecked his truck when night rain greased
the Cedar Creek pike.
People are dying by the hundreds in Rwanda,
but reality is the stricken faces
of the careless driver's grandparents:
lives which should be in order
shamed now by his recklessness, his brush with hereafter.
There are roads leading out of Cashiers,
but I need them not.
No more than a shipwrecked fool
needs trade winds
which would bear him back to a raging world
from paradise.

The Riches of the Nations

I have left my partner far upstream
working a hole where water, dark with depth,
slides past gray rock, squeezed up at an angle
by the ancient play of petulant gods.
Trout have risen, but refused
the best we presented them.
Impossible such small brains
could outsmart us
who are so well outfitted for the sport
in the latest breathable waders,
vests with tricks in every pocket,
and costly graphite rods.

Now the afternoon light slants through hemlocks
making the river translucent, almost as clear as gin, yet
fish can change color to match the amber gravel bottom,
and I cannot see whether any are holding in this run.
It is almost time to stop for the day.
Nothing the experts recommended has proved
a suitable offering for these finny challengers.

I reach into my silver metal fly box where feathery creations
nest in parallel rows of white foam
as if every insect you ever saw had scented overripe fruit
and alighted at the same time.

The one I select lands in a line of bubbles,
seems detached from the fine monofilament line.
Filling blanks in an imaginary matrix,
I place it in different grids until
the surface erupts with a tearing noise
like a bullfrog leaping into a weed-covered lake
as you walk with your lover on a sultry summer night.

The rainbow trout thrashes and runs
with primal ferocity.
I bring the creature in, beautiful in its wildness,
and return it unharmed to its rippling domain.

The fish has taught me again:
no matter what the day has gained or lost
it is worthy always to believe
in one more cast.

Necessary Servants

Vultures
somber in their ragged black feathers,
their two-note wing thrusts
like impatient fingers tapping a casket.
Great birds, dark as their daily work,
roost-bound in line through the blue
like students exiting the parking lot
at undertaker's college.

October Coins

How shall we spend the 31 gold coins of October,
this month of heart-quickening brass dawns,
tawny afternoons, and impossibly blue skies?
This time when slanting sunlight gilds harvested fields
and even poor men pause to count their wealth
before winter demands its tax.
The symbolism of changing leaves is inescapable:
it is the autumn of life as well.
My dead father's voice whispers
to lay by some of the money,
stay close to home, navigate familiar stairwells,
lest a misstep crack brittle bones, and
sip the rich chocolate of past adventures,
instead of seeking new ones.
Unlike many men, however, I am plagued in fall,
imagining that, even at my desk, I can sniff wisps
of acrid campfire smoke drifting toward the city
from hunting camps,
and smell the butternut essence of oiled leather rifle slings.
I long for the robust enthusiasm, the brotherhood
of men in camouflage who are drawn like iron filings
by an inexplicable magnetism far more ancient
than the memories of their distant ancestors.
Yes, I will risk all of October's coins
on one pull of the slot machine,
seeking three bell fruit bars for my soul.
I will be high in a tree when crisp mornings
let heavy-antlered bucks know it is time
to stalk stiff-legged from thickets where they hide and,
caution forgone, follow the wafting scent
of does in estrus
and plant in them the future.
February's bleak pewter days are soon enough
to deposit in an account for the future,
to come crawling back to my lover
begging forgiveness for the sportsman's wastrel life,
praying that she has not found a more attentive swain
as, in all too many Octobers past,
they have.

The Hope of Upstream Water

I have read the promises of Isaiah,
heard the broker's tout,
studied the racing form on ponies,
but this bright September morning,
the green river gurgling and pressing against my knees,
I seek salvation
in the hope of upstream water.
A cool gust showers leaves
on the stream. Little remains of my summer.
I loft prayers to heaven
in a whispering yellow curl of fly line
seeking that eddy by the boulder
where a fat brown trout may rest
waiting for caddis flies
like St. Peter pausing at the distant lamentation
of one more sinner
dashing to make the gate
before it closes for the day.
The line straightens like the life
of an old roué toward the end.
My imitation bug floats on an altar of stillness
waiting for the judgment
before the current sweeps it down.
If the fish takes it, today will have meaning
and maybe the misspent days before it,
and that would be redemption enough.

Another Imperfect Chapter

Soft mist tendrils rise from the lake
like Sioux villages signaling
success with the buffalo.
Bream are eager for the fluorescent green blob
at the end of my fly line.
At my approach
green egrets launch from shore grass,
loaf out across the water
on soundless wings
like the affection of women
I have not pursued artfully.
The sun rises kindly,
taking its time finding me
among the pines.
Six hen mallards paddle
from their reedy sanctuary, glaring
that I interrupted their morning gossip.
The clack of golf balls comes between
me and solitude like a righteous chaperone
flinging open a bedroom door.
Another imperfect chapter, but
not a bad place for a book
to end.

Acknowledgements

In 1990, I published a slim volume of my work entitled, *That Nature Might Stand Up.*

A number of respected persons have urged another book. So, here is a little collection, ostensibly on hunting, fishing, and outdoor work, but really on what these activities teach men about life, albeit much is yet to be learned.

It is dedicated to my family and friends in the hope that their holiday season will be even more special.

Someone said, "To expose your feelings is to risk exposing your true self." I have risked friendship repeatedly. As everyone knows, some friendships end sadly. Most, however, have brought profound joy.

Several of these poems have been blessed with awards. Your enjoyment will be their supreme blessing.

Special thanks to Roy Conradi, Conradi Communications,for the cover design, Jimmy Nygaard at Sewell Printing Service for his expertise, counsel, and unerringly courteous companionship afield, to Tammy Eigel at Longstreet Press for help on the ISBN, and to Elizabeth Griffin and Cathy Ottley for careful proofreading.

John Ottley, Jr.

December, 1999